Yellow

A Blast from the Past

by Donna Richardson

Harcourt
SCHOOL PUBLISHERS

Cover, p.3, ©PhotoDisc/Punch Stock; p.5, p.9, ©Corbis; p.6, ©PhotoDisc; p.7, p.8, ©National Park Service; p.10, (tr) ©John C. Stevenson/Animals Animals, (l) ©National Park Service; p.11, (tl) ©Leonard Rue Enterprises/Animals Animals, (r) ©Theo Alloffs/Visuals Unlimited; p.12, ©Kennan Ward/CORBIS; p.13, ©Toyohiro Yamada/Getty Images; p.14, ©Lewis Kemper/Stone/Getty Images.

Cartography, p.4, Joe LeMonnier

Printed in China

ISBN 10: 0-15-350988-0
ISBN 13: 978-0-15-350988-9

Ordering Options
ISBN 10: 0-15-350601-6 (Grade 4 On-Level Collection)
ISBN 13: 978-0-15-350601-7 (Grade 4 On-Level Collection)
ISBN 10: 0-15-357941-2 (package of 5)
ISBN 13: 978-0-15-357941-7 (package of 5)

4 5 6 7 8 9 10 0940 12 11 10 09

The morning sun peeks out over a landscape that has been much the same for thousands of years. Mountains and valleys stretch for miles. Ancient forests have trees that have turned to stone. Pine forests are homes to bears, squirrels, and chipmunks. Through the trees, visitors can hear the hissing of spouting water. The land is called Yellowstone National Park.

Yellowstone is a magnificent place. There are many waterfalls cascading into deep canyons of rock. Herds of bison dot the land. Elk graze in the green fields. Moose and deer wade through flowing streams.

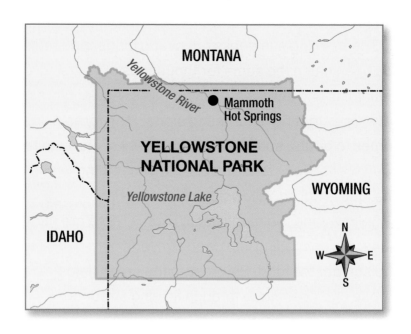

Each year millions of visitors from all over the world make the trip to Yellowstone National Park, located mostly in the state of Wyoming. Yellowstone became the world's first national park in 1872.

A visit to the park helps people understand many of the forces that take place in the Earth. The wonders at Yellowstone were formed millions of years ago when a huge volcano erupted. Ash covered much of the western United States. The eruption left a hole in the ground 30 miles (48 km) long and 45 miles (72 km) wide. This huge hole was the beginning of Yellowstone.

The land took shape over many millions of years. Visitors today can see the results of the great volcanic eruptions that happened millions of years ago. Hot springs bubble with steaming water that rises through the cracks of rocks. Visitors walking through these parts of the park must walk along roped off paths. To walk near the hot springs could be dangerous!

Pools of water have formed in some of these hot springs. The clear water glistens. The bottoms of some pools of water are lined with sulfur, a yellow substance found in the Earth. The blue water and yellow sulfur make the pool a sparkling green.

Visitors may first stop at one of the park's most famous spots, Old Faithful, only one of Yellowstone's thousands of geysers. A geyser is an underground hot spring in which water boils. The pressure from the boiling water regularly sends a column of hot water high into the air.

Visitors to Yellowstone will see more geysers here than anywhere on Earth. Old Faithful goes off about every sixty to ninety minutes. Each time, it sprays its steaming water high into the air for several minutes. Visitors gather around Old Faithful to see the event. People have fun trying to predict the exact moment Old Faithful will let off its powerful hot water stream high up into the air.

Bubbling mudpots

Visitors might next go to see some of Yellowstone's bubbling mudpots. To do so, visitors walk on a wooden path along Grand Loop Road. Here, mud bubbles and boils in the ground. Some bubbles are as big as soccer balls! When they burst, globs of mud spurt into the air. Visitors are not allowed off the path for their own safety. Flying hot globs of mud could burn people.

On top of Roaring Mountain, visitors hear the hissing of hot steam as it escapes from vents in the Earth. Roaring Mountain got its name from the loud roaring sounds that come from these vents. It's almost as if a snoring giant sleeps below the ground.

Yellowstone Park is not all bubbling, steaming, boiling land. Pine trees and forests cover many parts of the park. People spend their days hiking along any of thousands of trails. Hiking is one way that visitors can see the interesting animal and plant life of the park.

Visitors must be careful as they walk. They would not want to surprise a sleeping bear along the way. Park rangers warn visitors not to feed the bears. Many of the bears appear tame, but they are still dangerous. The most dangerous animal in the park is the grizzly bear. It is important to take the rangers' warnings about bears seriously!

A herd of bison

One of the most interesting animals of Yellowstone
is the bison. Bison have been living in the land of
Yellowstone for millions of years. At one point, they
were almost extinct. Less than fifty bison were left
here in the park. Now thousands of bison can be seen
across the grasslands and meadows.

Large herds of elk also graze in the grasses of
the park. Rangers warn visitors to remain distant from
these large animals because elk have been known to
ram into cars with their enormous antlers.

Bighorn sheep

Moose

If visitors pay close attention, they might be able to spot a moose in the willows. Moose are a rare sight in Yellowstone. Moose are different from bison or elk because bison and elk move in herds. Moose are most likely spotted alone or in pairs.

Lucky visitors may also see bighorn sheep. These animals, known for their huge curved horns, can be seen climbing the steep sides of mountains. During the mating season, male sheep butt heads with each other. The noise they make can be heard from far away.

Many of Yellowstone's animals are predators, animals that hunt other animals for food. Visitors will probably not see these animals out in the open. Many hunt during the early hours of the morning or near sunset.

Bobcat

Lynx

One such animal, the bobcat, is a small wild cat.
It has reddish-brown fur with black stripes and spots.
Bobcats live along rocky cliffs or in pine forests. They
hunt smaller animals such as rabbits, hares, mice,
and young deer.

Another wildcat that visitors rarely see is the lynx.
Park rangers think there are very few lynx in the park.
Lynx look a lot like bobcats. If a visitor spots either
one of these animals, the park rangers want to know
about it. This helps them understand more about
these animals.

Many years ago, there were few wolves in the park. People were allowed to hunt wolves because the wolves hunted and killed the park's elk. Then people realized that the hunters had upset the balance of nature. Without wolves, there were too many elk in the park. It became hard for the elk to find food. Park rangers worked hard to bring wolves back to Yellowstone. Now many more wolves live there.

Wolves live in groups called packs. A wolf most likely will not attack a visitor, but it might if a visitor gets too close to its young. Wolves protect and guard their young like sentries.

Another interesting thing to do is visit Old Fort Yellowstone. There visitors see how soldiers lived at Yellowstone one hundred years ago. People can even take a ride in an old-time horse-drawn carriage!

Visitors will want to see some of the park's many waterfalls. The Lower Falls is the tallest waterfall in the park. This waterfall rises to a height of over 300 feet (91 m). Visitors can watch the waters from a wooden platform above the falls. The falls have changed over the years due to the rushing water eroding the rocks below. The rushing water will continue to change the shape of the falls in the future.

At the end of the day, weary visitors return to camp. They have spent the day hearing the wind in the trees and the bubbling of streams and mudpots. The sights of hissing, steaming water from the geysers and hot springs will be forever embedded in visitors' minds. They may have smelled the fresh scent of pine from forests or perhaps the stinky sulfur from the Earth!

Nowhere else in the world is quite like Yellowstone National Park. Visitors rest in their camps at night and watch the sun set over the park as it has for millions of years. Some may even dream about the wonderful sights they saw in Yellowstone Park.

Think Critically

1. What kinds of natural sights can a person see in Yellowstone?

2. Why do you think that Yellowstone was made into a national park?

3. Why do you think Old Faithful is called that?

4. Why do you think the author wrote this book? How do you know?

5. What part of Yellowstone would you most like to see?

 Science

Find Out More Use a book or the Internet to find out more information about geysers. What causes them? Where are they located? Write a paragraph or two reporting your findings.

School-Home Connection Tell family members what you learned from this book about Yellowstone National Park. Then find out about other interesting national parks.